The Complete Heart Healthy Cookbook for Beginners 2023

2000 Days of Low Sodium & Low Fat Recipes to Improve your Heart Health | 30-Day Meal Plan to Lower Blood Pressure and Cholesterol Levels

Ethan Lambert

Table of Contents

WHAT IS HEART DISEASES

Atherosclerosis is a process linked to many of the issues included in the heart and blood vessel disease category, usually referred to simply as heart disease. Plaque is a substance that builds up in the walls of the arteries and can lead to atherosclerosis, a condition that can lead to heart disease. This deposit causes the streets to become narrower, which makes it more difficult for blood to pass through. If a blood clot forms, it has the potential to obstruct the flow of blood. This has the potential to bring on a heart attack or a stroke.

A person is said to have suffered a heart attack when a blood clot prevents blood from reaching a portion of the heart. If this clot entirely obstructs the flow of blood, the amount of the heart muscle that is fed by the affected artery will start to die. Most people with a heart attack will survive it and lead regular lives, during which they will have many more years during which they will be productive. However, having a heart attack does mean you need to make certain lifestyle adjustments. Your doctor will recommend drugs and adjustments to your lifestyle that are appropriate for you based on the extent of the damage to your heart and the severity of the heart disease that led to the heart attack.

Ischemic strokes are the most common, and they occur when a blood vessel that supplies blood to the brain becomes blocked, typically due to a blood clot. Brain cells will perish if they are deprived of oxygen and nutrients from the blood supply to their brain region. Consequently, the individual won't be able to do some of the duties they were previously capable of, such as walking or talking. When a blood vessel within the brain breaks, a person will suffer from a hemorrhagic stroke. Uncontrolled hypertension is the most likely contributing factor (blood pressure).

If too many brain cells die due to a stroke due to a lack of blood and oxygen reaching the brain, then some of the stroke symptoms are permanent. These cells do not get replaced at any point. The good news is that some brain cells don't die; instead, they are merely temporarily malfunctioning. Damaged cells can repair themselves. Some of the body's functions get better as time goes on and the damage is repaired.

Additionally, other brain cells might take Control of the portions of the brain that have been damaged. Strength may increase as a result of this, as may fluency in speech, and memory improvement may also result. The recovery process lies at the heart of what it means to undergo rehabilitation.

WHAT ARE THE CAUSES OF HEART DISEASE?

Unhealthy lifestyle choices, such as a lack of physical activity, tobacco products, or an unhealthy diet, often bring on heart disease. Age, gender, and the medical history of one's family all play a significant part in the equation. Infections or genetic abnormalities that damage the heart can also lead to heart disease, which is not tied to people's choices regarding their lifestyle.

High blood cholesterol, diabetes, high blood pressure, and obesity are illnesses caused by poor diet and lifestyle inactivity. These conditions frequently serve as precursors to cardiovascular disease.

Plaque can form in the walls of blood vessels when high blood cholesterol is commonly caused by eating a diet high in fat. Plaque formation is a condition that has no associated symptoms but can lead to a constriction of the arteries, an increase in blood pressure, and even an unexpected episode of heart failure.

Other Forms of Cardiovascular Disease

Heart failure: If you have heart failure, this does not necessarily mean your heart will stop beating. Heart failure, also known as congestive heart failure, is a condition that occurs when the heart is unable to pump blood as effectively as it should. Even if it is still beating, the heart cannot satisfy the body's demands for blood and oxygen. If treatment is not received, heart failure may become even more severe. If a member of your family has heart failure, you must follow the instructions given by the doctor.

Arrhythmia: An arrhythmia is a condition in which the heart beats in an abnormal rhythm. There is a wide variety of abnormal heartbeats known as arrhythmias. The seat can beat too slowly, too quickly, or even in an irregular pattern. When the heart rate is lower than 60 beats per minute, a condition known as bradycardia exists. A condition known as tachycardia exists when the heart beats at a rate greater than 100 times per minute. The efficiency with which the heart pumps blood can be negatively impacted by arrhythmia. The core may not pump enough blood to satisfy the body's requirements.

Heart valve problems: Problems with the heart valves. Stenosis is the medical term used to describe the condition when the heart valves do not open fully, restricting blood flow through the heart. Regurgitation is the term used to describe a requirement in which the heart valves fail to close completely, allowing blood to back up into the heart's chambers. The disorder known as prolapse describes what happens when the valve leaflets bulge or prolapse back into the upper room.

Risk factors of heart disease

Those risk factors for heart disease are modifiable by modifying one's lifestyle and receiving preventative medical care regularly. The following are examples of risk variables that can be managed.

Obesity

People who are obese have a higher risk of developing high blood pressure, which raises the overall amount of work that needs to be done by the heart. They also tend to have high cholesterol levels, which increases the risk of creating a blockage in the blood flow to the heart. In addition, they are more likely to have a history of cardiovascular disease. In addition, being obese raises a person's risk of getting diabetes, another critical factor contributing to heart disease development. Some of the most effective strategies for preventing obesity and the health problems that come along with it include maintaining a nutritious diet and maintaining a regular exercise routine. Your doctor should analyze and treat any issues brought on by obesity.

High Cholesterol

High Cholesterol is a sort of lipid molecule that plays a vital role in maintaining healthy cell membranes. As such, Cholesterol plays an essential role in maintaining a healthy body. However, having excessive Cholesterol in your blood puts you at an elevated risk of developing heart disease. Atherosclerosis, a condition in which fatty plaques build up on the walls of blood vessels, restricts blood flow to the heart, and can ultimately cause a heart attack, can be caused by high Cholesterol levels and other fatty substances.

There are two different kinds of Cholesterol: LDL, also known as "bad cholesterol," and HDL, also known as "good cholesterol" (the "good" Cholesterol). Your risk of having a heart attack is raised when your LDL cholesterol levels are high. In contrast, having a higher level of HDLs confers a higher degree of protection against the rate of heart attacks. Several factors, including your age, gender, genetics, dietary habits, and level of physical activity, influence your cholesterol levels. It is possible to lower LDL cholesterol by engaging in physical activity and altering one's diet, such as avoiding saturated and trans fats. Exercising is the most effective technique to improve your "good" (HDL) cholesterol levels.

Modifications to your diet and your level of physical activity can help lower your Cholesterol. Still, suppose your levels cannot be maintained at a safe level (the ideal number depends on your family history, age, and medical histories such as diabetes or a history of heart attacks). In that case, you and your doctor may want to discuss the possibility of a prescription for cholesterol-lowering medications. People with a family history of diabetes or heart attacks have a more outstanding obligation to maintain a lower level of LDL cholesterol than those who do not have such a family history.

Cigarette smoking

Cigarette smoking is one of the most critical risk factors for heart attacks. Smoking elevates blood pressure and makes people's blood clot more easily, both of which put a person's heart in danger and are among the many adverse effects of smoking on one's health. If you want to reduce your risk of developing heart disease, the most significant thing you can do for yourself is to either never start smoking or quit smoking entirely if you already do.

High Blood Pressure

The risk of developing heart disease increases when blood pressure is not kept under Control. If your blood pressure is high, it will be more difficult for your heart to circulate blood throughout the rest of your body. An overworked heart responds to physical activity in the same way as other strained muscles do by enlarging itself, expressly by increasing the thickness of its walls and its overall volume. Even though these adjustments appear beneficial, they are dangerous and are symptoms of heart disease. The thickening of the heart's walls results in a significant reduction in the volume of the heart chamber, resulting in a decreased capacity for the heart to pump blood with each beat. Additionally, because the muscle walls have become thicker, it is more difficult for the heart to pump out the blood that it has been able to gather. Eating well, Exercising regularly, and taking prescribed medicine (where necessary) are all ways to assist in the upkeep of healthy blood pressure and, by extension, a healthy heart.

Diabetes

As was just said, diabetes is a crucial contributor to the risk of developing heart disease. If a person has diabetes, their risk of acquiring heart disease is comparable to the danger posed by someone who has already suffered a heart attack. Diabetes is a condition that affects the regulation of blood sugar. Those with diabetes are more likely to develop cardiovascular disease if they cannot effectively manage their blood sugar levels. In addition, people with diabetes are responsible for maintaining normal levels of blood pressure and Cholesterol in their bodies. The target level of Cholesterol for a person with diabetes is the same as that for a person who has already suffered a heart attack.

Other Considerations

Research has shown that depression, excessive alcohol consumption, and stress are all risk factors for cardiovascular disease. Stress may induce some people to overeat, smoke, or drink more than they should. Consuming alcohol is associated with an increased risk of high blood pressure and weight gain. There is a delicate balance to be struck here, even though some research suggests that a daily moderate alcohol intake (one drink per day) can lower the chance of developing heart disease. Alcohol is a drug that has the potential to be addictive, and it is also a source of "empty" calories, which are calories that have little to no nutritious value. These additional calories can lead to issues with weight gain and diabetes, both of which are independently linked to an increased risk of heart disease. It is essential to see your physician before making any choices regarding your alcohol consumption about the health of your heart.

WHAT IS A HEART-HEALTHY DIET?

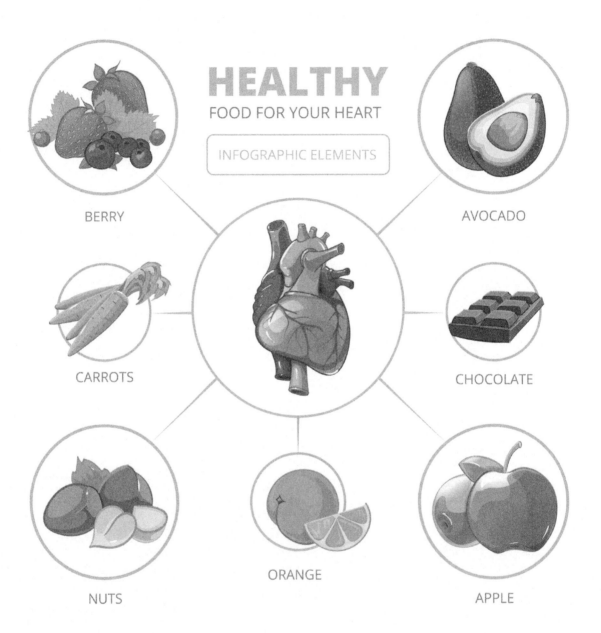

HEALTHY
FOOD FOR YOUR HEART

INFOGRAPHIC ELEMENTS

BERRY

AVOCADO

CARROTS

CHOCOLATE

NUTS

ORANGE

APPLE

Heart disease is the leading cause of death for men and women and is responsible for more deaths than all types of cancer. The emotional toll of receiving a diagnosis of cardiovascular disease can be significant, and it can affect a person's mood, quality of life, and attitude. In addition to maintaining a healthy weight and engaging in regular physical activity, maintaining a healthy heart also requires paying attention to the foods you consume regularly. Consuming foods that are good for your kindness and leading a healthy lifestyle may reduce your risk of cardiovascular disease and stroke by as much as 80 percent.

Because no one meal can miraculously make you healthy, your entire dietary pattern is more significant than the foods you consume individually. A diet that is good for the heart consists of "real," natural food that is obtained in its most natural state, such as food that has not been processed, deep-fried or packaged, as well as meals and snacks that are low in sugar.

These tips for a heart-healthy diet can help you better manage conditions such as high Cholesterol and high blood pressure, whether you are trying to improve your cardiovascular health, have already been diagnosed with heart disease, are trying to improve your cardiovascular health, or are looking to lower your risk of having a heart attack.

HEART-HEALTHY DIET: STEPS TO PREVENT HEART DISEASE

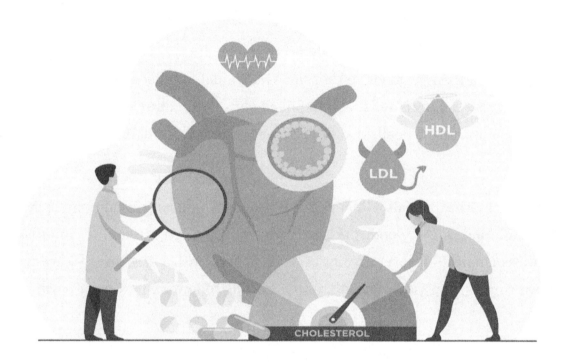

A healthy diet for the heart is the first step in preventing heart disease. Are you prepared to begin your diet to protect your heart? The following are tips to help you get started.

Even if you know that consuming some foods can raise your risk of developing heart disease, changing your typical eating routine can be challenging. Here are suggestions for a healthy diet for the heart, which you may use whether you have spent years eating poorly or want to adjust your diet. You will be well on your way toward a good diet for your heart once you understand which foods you should eat more and which foods you should eat less.

1. CONTROL YOUR PORTION SIZE

How much food you consume is just as crucial as what you eat. It's possible to consume more calories than you should if you pile too much food on your plate, go back for seconds, and keep eating until you feel full. Restaurant portions are typically far more significant than the average person's requirement.

If you restrict the amount of food you eat by following a few easy guidelines, you can improve your diet, cardiovascular health, and waistline.

If you're having trouble controlling your servings, try using a smaller dish or bowl.

Consume more foods high in nutrients yet low in calories, such as fruits and vegetables.

Consume fewer calories and sodium from meals that are refined, processed, or obtained from fast food restaurants, and do so in smaller portions.

You must keep track of the number of servings you consume at all times. Several factors to keep in mind are as follows:

A serving size is a predetermined quantity of food, usually expressed in standard units of measurement like cups, ounces, or pieces. For instance, one serving of spaghetti is approximately one-third to one-half cup, roughly the size of a hockey puck. A single serving of beef, fish, or chicken is around 2 to 3 ounces, comparable in size and depth to a standard deck of playing cards.

The number of servings recommended for each food group may change depending on your diet or set of guidelines.

The ability to judge portion size must be mastered. Until you are confident in your ability to evaluate quantities, you might find it necessary to use a scale, measuring cups and spoons, or both.

2. EAT MORE VEGETABLES AND FRUITS

Fruits and vegetables are excellent for receiving daily vitamins and minerals. Both fruits and vegetables contain relatively few calories and are excellent sources of nutritional fiber. Vegetables and fruits, along with other plant-based foods and meals derived from plants, include chemicals hypothesized to be beneficial in preventing cardiovascular disease. It's possible that increasing your intake of fruits and vegetables will make it easier for you to reduce your consumption of foods that are higher in calories, such as meat, cheese, and snack foods.

Including fruits and veggies in your diet doesn't have to be complicated. Stock your refrigerator with washed and chopped vegetables for easy access to healthy snacks. Keep a bowl of fruit in your kitchen so that you will be reminded to consume it throughout the day. Pick meals in which vegetables or fruits are the primary components, such as vegetable stir-fry or salads that combine fresh fruit into the mix.

The best vegetables and fruits to choose	Limit your intake of vegetables and fruits
<ul><li>Vegetables and fruits that are both fresh and frozen</li><li>Vegetables canned with low sodium</li><li>Juice- or water-packed canned fruit</li></ul>	<ul><li>Coconut</li><li>The vegetables should be paired with creamy sauces</li><li>Vegetables that are fried or breaded</li><li>Heavy syrup-packed canned fruit</li><li>Frozen fruit flavored with sugar</li></ul>

3. GO FOR THE ENTIRE GRAINS.

Whole grains are excellent providers of fiber as well as other nutrients that help maintain heart health and healthy blood pressure. It is possible to boost the proportion of whole grains in a diet beneficial for the heart by making simple substitutes for products that include refined grains. You may also go out on a limb and experiment with new whole grains, such as whole-grain farro, quinoa, or barley.

Choosing the right grain products	Limiting or avoiding grain products
• *Flour made from whole wheat* • *Bread made from whole grains, preferably whole wheat or whole grain bread* • *Cereals with 5 grams or more of fiber per serving* • *There are many healthy whole grains out there, such as brown rice, barley, and buckwheat (kasha).* • *Whole-grain pasta* • *Regular or steel-cut oatmeal*	• *Cornbread* • *Cakes* • *Pies* • *Muffins* • *White, refined flour* • *White bread* • *High-fat snack crackers* • *Frozen waffles* • *Buttered popcorn* • *Egg noodles* • *Doughnuts* • *Biscuits* • *Quick bread*

4. REDUCE YOUR INTAKE OF HARMFUL FATS

If you want to lower your blood cholesterol and lessen your risk of coronary artery disease, one vital step you can take is to cut back on the amount of saturated and trans fats in your diet. Atherosclerosis, also known as hardening of the arteries, is a condition that can be brought on by having excessive levels of Cholesterol in the blood. This condition can make a person more susceptible to a heart attack or a stroke.

The American Heart Association provides the following recommendations for how much fat should be included in a diet that is healthy for the heart:

Fat type	Recommendation
Saturated fat	It represents about 11 to 13 grams of carbohydrates per day if you eat 2,000 calories a day.
Trans fat	Avoid

The Dietary Guidelines for Americans 2020-2025 recommend keeping the amount of saturated fat in one's diet to less than ten percent of the total calories consumed daily.

There are several simple methods available for reducing the intake of saturated and trans fats:

Remove excess fat from meat or select lean cuts of beef that contain less than 10 percent fat.

When cooking and serving, reduce the amount of butter, margarine, and shortening.

For a healthy diet for the heart, make replacements lower in fat whenever possible. As an alternative to butter, you could, for instance spread low-sugar fruit spread or sliced whole fruit over toast in place of margarine. Another option would be to top a baked potato with low-sodium salsa or low-fat yogurt.

Check the ingredient lists behind crackers, chips, cookies, and frosting packages. These items not only have a low nutritional value, but some of them, especially those marketed as having decreased fat, may contain trans fats. There is a possibility that older items may still include trans fats in them even though trans fats cannot legally be added to foods anymore. On the ingredient label, trans fats might be placed under the more general category of partly hydrogenated oil.

Fats to choose	Fats to limit
• Canola oil • Margarine, trans-fat-free • Cholesterol-lowering margarine, such as Benecol, Promise Activ or Smart Balance • Vegetable and nut oils • Nuts, seeds • Olive oil • Avocados	• Hydrogenated margarine and shortening • Bacon fat • Gravy • Cream sauce • Butter • Nondairy creamers • Cocoa butter, found in chocolate • Lard • Coconut, palm, cottonseed and palm kernel oils

When you do use fats, use monounsaturated fats like olive oil or canola oil instead of saturated fats like butter or margarine. A diet low in saturated fat and high in monounsaturated fat, such as the Mediterranean diet, has been shown to reduce the risk of coronary heart disease. Monounsaturated and polyunsaturated fats, when consumed in place of saturated fat, can assist in lowering total blood cholesterol. However, it is necessary to exercise moderation. There is no single form of fat that is not heavy in calories.

Using ground flaxseed is a simple method to incorporate healthful fat (as well as fiber) into your diet. Flaxseeds are a type of seed that are tiny and brown. They are rich in fiber as well as omega-3 fatty acids. According to several studies, flaxseed can help reduce harmful levels of Cholesterol in some people. You can grind the flaxseeds in a coffee grinder or a food processor and then add 5 mL of the ground flaxseeds to one serving of yogurt, applesauce, or hot porridge.

5. SELECT PROTEIN SOURCES THAT ARE LOW IN FAT.

Eggs, lean cuts of meat, poultry, and fish, as well as fish and poultry with low-fat content, are some of the best protein sources. Choose lower-fat options, such as skinless chicken breasts rather than fried chicken patties and skim milk rather than whole milk. These substitutions will help you reduce the amount of saturated fat you consume.

Fish is a healthy alternative to meats that are higher in fat. Triglycerides are blood fats, and certain varieties of fish are exceptionally high in omega-3 fatty acids, which have been shown to reduce their levels. Cold-water fish, such as salmon, mackerel, and herring, contain the most elevated omega-3 fatty acids than any other type of fish. In addition to these foods, walnuts, soybeans, flaxseed, and canola oil are good sources.

In addition to being fantastic, low-fat protein sources, legumes, which include beans, peas, and lentils, do not contain any cholesterol, making them an excellent meat substitute. When you eat a plant-based protein instead of an animal-based protein, such as a soy or bean burger instead of a hamburger, you will consume less fat and Cholesterol while consuming more fiber.

Choosing the right protein	Limiting or avoiding proteins
• Fish, especially fatty, cold-water fish such as salmon • Skinless poultry • Soybeans and soy products, such as soy burgers and tofu • Lean ground meats • Yogurt, cheese, and skim milk with a fat content of 1 percent or less • Eggs • Legumes	• Dairy products and full-fat milk • Spareribs • Fatty and marbled meats • Bacon • Hot dogs and sausages • Organ meats, such as liver • Fried or breaded meats

6. LIMIT OR DECREASE SALT (SODIUM)

Consuming excessive salt can raise blood pressure, a risk factor for cardiovascular disease. A diet low in salt (sodium) is an essential component of a healthy diet for the heart. The American Heart Association suggests the following, which should be followed:

The daily sodium intake for healthy persons should not exceed 2,300 milligrams (mg) (about a teaspoon of salt)

It is recommended that most adults consume no more than 1,500 milligrams of sodium daily.

Even though lowering the amount of salt that is added to meals at the table or while it is being prepared is a good beginning step, the majority of the salt that you consume comes from foods that have been canned or processed, such as baked goods, frozen dinners, and soups. Consuming fresh foods and preparing your soups and stews at home are two ways to reduce the amount of salt you take daily.

If the convenience of canned soups and ready-made meals appeals to you, seek varieties with no added salt or decreased sodium levels. Be skeptical of goods that claim to have a lower sodium content because they are seasoned with sea salt rather than the common table salt that is typically used. Sea salt has the same nutritional value as conventional table salt.

Another thing you can do to lower the amount of salt in your diet is to be selective about the condiments you use. Numerous herbs can be purchased in forms with less salt. Salt replacements can give your food more taste while reducing the amount of salt it contains.

Choose low-salt items	Avoid or limit high-salt items
<ul><li>Salted-reduced versions of condiments, such as ketchup and soy sauce.</li><li>Herbs and spices</li><li>Salt-free seasoning blends</li><li>Salt-free or reduced-salt canned soups and prepared meals</li></ul>	<ul><li>Various condiments such as ketchup, mayonnaise, and soy sauce</li><li>Restaurant meals</li><li>Table salt</li><li>Ready-to-eat foods, such as frozen dinners and canned soups</li><li>Tomato juice</li></ul>

7. PREPARE IN ADVANCE: MAKE MENUS FOR EACH DAY.

Create your daily menus using the above six different approaches. Emphasize foods high in vegetables, fruits, and whole grains when choosing foods for each meal and snack. Choose lean sources of protein and healthy fats, and cut out on meals high in salt. Be mindful of the proportions of your portions, and strive to offer a diverse selection of foods.

For instance, if you grilled fish for dinner one night, you may try a burger made with black beans the next night. This makes it more likely that you will consume all the necessary nutrients for your body. Adding variety to meals and snacks is another way to make them more attractive.

8. REWARD YOURSELF EVERY ONCE IN A WHILE.

Every once in a while, it would help if you treated yourself to something luxurious. Your efforts to maintain a healthy diet for your heart won't be undone by a single candy bar or a handful of potato chips. However, you should not let this excuse you to abandon your plan to eat healthy foods. You will be able to maintain a healthy lifestyle in the long run if instances of overindulgence are the exception rather than the rule. The most important thing is to ensure that most of your meals consist of nutritious foods.

If you implement these tips into your lifestyle, you'll find that maintaining a diet that's good for your heart is not only possible but also fun. You can eat with your heart in mind if you plan and make a few simple alternatives.

BENEFITS OF EATING A HEART-HEALTHY DIET

Eating food with a focus on keeping your heart healthy has several positive effects. The following are some of them:

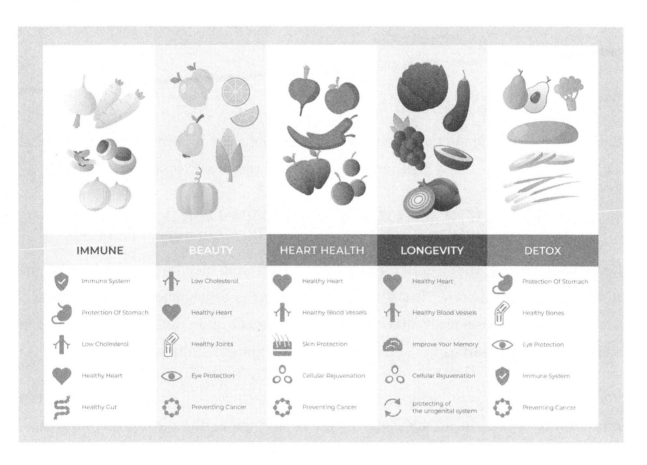

1. BRING DOWN YOUR BLOOD PRESSURE

A good diet for your heart can positively affect your blood pressure, blood sugars, and triglycerides. If you are concerned about high blood pressure or a condition that causes blood sugar swings, such as diabetes, then changing your diet to be more heart-healthy could also improve those issues. This is because a heart-healthy diet is more likely to contain foods low in saturated and monounsaturated fat.

The DASH plan, which stands for "dietary approaches to stop hypertension," is one that the medical staff at Ross Bridge Medical Center frequently suggests to patients who suffer from high blood pressure. The DASH diet prioritizes the following aspects:

Limiting sodium intake

reducing intake of saturated fats

Reducing sugar intake

Eating more foods high in potassium, calcium, and magnesium, which are nutrients that actively help regulate blood pressure, can lower your risk of developing hypertension.

2. LOWER YOUR CHOLESTEROL RATINGS

Cholesterol can clog your arteries, responsible for carrying blood from your heart to the rest of your body's tissues. This, in turn, can lead to the development of a heart attack. About one person has a heart attack every forty seconds here in the United States. A diet beneficial to one's heart can, thankfully, assist in bringing cholesterol levels down.

Reduced consumption of saturated and trans fats, which can frequently be found in processed foods, red meat, and dairy products, are among the dietary solutions used. These fats ought to be changed out for monounsaturated and polyunsaturated fats, which may be found in sunflower oil, olive oil, avocados, and nuts.

Consuming extra fiber, such as that found in beans, oats, flaxseed, apples, and citrus fruits can also assist in the reduction of cholesterol levels in the body.

3. REDUCE YOUR WAISTLINE

Taking the necessary precautions to protect your heart, such as eating a healthy diet and being active for at least 150 minutes of activity each week at a moderate intensity, can also affect your waistline. You can improve the health of your heart and enjoy a slim figure if you exercise and pay attention to what you eat.

4. RAISE THE ENERGY LEVELS IN YOUR BODY

If your heart is healthy, you may also have more energy. And foods that can help keep your heart healthy, such as nuts, avocados, olives, lean meat, seeds, fish, whole grains, fruits, and vegetables, can give your heart the vitamins, minerals, and nutrients it needs while also helping you stay energized at the same time. These foods include nuts, seeds, avocados, olives, lean meat, fish, whole grains, fruits, and vegetables.

5. EXPAND YOUR POTENTIAL FOR LONGEVITY

Worldwide, coronary heart disease is the leading cause of death for both men and women. In addition, coronary heart disease is responsible for the end of one out of every four people in the United States.

Therefore, if you can enhance your heart health by changing the foods you consume, you can increase your longevity and extend the length of your life.

Eating foods that are good for you is essential for every household member. Maintaining a healthy balance in one's diet by eating everything in moderation is the most important thing. Eating in the style of the Mediterranean region is considered to preserve your heart (i.e., protects your heart and blood vessels). A diet that is considered to be Mediterranean is characterized by the consumption of a great deal of fruit and vegetables, whole grains, olive oil, whole grains, fish, a moderate amount of wine, eating with one's family and friends, and activities that help one to relax and calm down. The following are some of the primary tenets of the Mediterranean diet that, when adhered to, can have positive effects not only on one's heart health but also on their general state of health.

THE SEVEN-DAY PLAN FOR A HEART-SMART DIET

A diet that is good for your heart should include lean proteins and low-fat dairy products, unsaturated fats, tons of fresh fruit and vegetables, and plenty of fiber. Here is a seven-day meal plan to help you follow a good diet for your heart. Additionally, it is simple to understand. Because this meal plan is based on around 1,800 calories, if your doctor advises you to lose weight, you may need to reduce the size of your portions and eliminate some foods from your diet. If, on the other hand, you are maintaining your current weight (or you could stand to gain a few pounds), you should up the quantities of lean proteins and add some additional olive oil, fruits, and vegetables to your diet.

MENU PLAN FOR THE NEXT SEVEN DAYS

Breakfast choices include:

Day 1

Oatmeal and fruit for breakfast.

The following amounts are recommended: 1 serving of oats (118mL dry oatmeal), cooked with water, 90mL raisins, 1 banana, or 1 and a half cups of fruits or vegetables, topped with 15mL ground flaxseeds. After this, one slice of whole-wheat toast spread with stanol or plant sterol margarine (for example, Benecol or Take Control).

Day 2

Cereal, milk, and fruit.

The serving should contain 235 mL of high-fiber cereal (any brand that contains 5+ mL of fiber and 120 calories or fewer per serving) — 235 mL of skim, 1% low-fat milk or soymilk — plus one fruit (12 bananas, 235 mL of berries, or 30 mL of raisins) — plus 1 slice of whole-wheat toast spread with plant sterols or stanol margarine — and 1 serving of any (e.g., Benecol).

Day 3

A serving of fruit is served with toast with tomato slices and low or nonfat cheese.

A serving of any fruit, one serving of whole-wheat bread, two slices of melted low- or nonfat cheese, and two slices of tomato slices.

Day 4

Omelette made using egg whites.

You can prepare two slices of whole-wheat toast smeared with plant sterol or stanol margarine and a side of nonstick cooking spray by frying five egg whites or a small container of egg substitute with whatever vegetables you like (for example, onion, tomato, and pepper). As an alternative, you might consider eating a fruit portion.

Day 5

Yogurt and fruit.

You can add one serving of any fruit, thirty mL of ground flaxseeds, and thirty mL of wheat germ with one slice of whole-wheat toast and a spread of plant sterol/stanol margarine to one container (8 ounces) of nonfat, flavored yogurt (or 235 mL of cottage cheese with one percent fat) combined.

Day 6

Toast/tomato/salmon with fruit.

Sandwich made with two slices of whole-wheat toast topped with thinly sliced tomatoes, salmon, and light cream cheese. A fruit portion is also included.

Day 7

Smoothie made with soymilk and fruit.

The following ingredients are blended in a blender until smooth: frozen strawberries, soymilk, bananas, and ice cubes. Two teaspoons of natural peanut butter spread on one slice of whole wheat toast.

Breakfast beverages:

Obviously, coffee or tea with nonfat milk and water. Avoid all fruit juices at all costs.

Choose one of the following for a morning snack option:

- A piece of low-fat cheese or tofu cheese, along with a piece of fruit
- Peanut butter topped with one apple slice
- Bags of oatmeal bran pretzels.
- The weight of each walnut or almond should be one ounce
- The following yogurts are available in 240 mL containers:
- 30 mL of hummus accompanied by 235 mL of baby carrots
- There is a big pear in the picture

Food for thought

Aspirin should be taken every day at a modest dose if you're at risk for heart disease. Blood clots can be prevented by taking aspirin. It is always a good idea to speak with your primary care provider before trying anything new.

Lunch

Day 1

The first day's meal was soup and pita bread.

You will need to avoid soups containing cheese, cream, or whole milk (about 2 cups) - try tomato, minestrone, lentil, chicken noodle, vegetarian chili, tomato rice, etc. A whole wheat pita bread and a vegetable salad with 5 mL of olive oil and unlimited vinegar topped with 15 mL of vinaigrette dressing.

Day 2

Sandwich and salad.

You may decide to serve it with three to five ounces of lean turkey breast, grilled chicken, lean ham, or low-fat tuna salad on two slices of whole-wheat or rye bread. Sandwiches with low-fat cheese are best complemented with lettuce, tomatoes, mustard, ketchup, barbecue sauce, or low-fat mayonnaise. This will be accompanied by one side salad dressed with 15 mL of vinaigrette (or unlimited olive oil and vinegar).

Day 3

Fish and vegetables grilled.

3-5 minutes on a grill or barbecue (without the skin), a side of steamed or softly cooked vegetables (2 cups) and a medium sweet potato. If you prefer grilled fish, you can use any fish that has been grilled. We will have a Japanese meal on day four, which includes a salad with ginger dressing (don't add too much), edamame (soybean sprouts), four pieces of sushi and five pieces of sashimi. If you wish to use soy sauce, make sure it has a reduced sodium content and use fresh ginger generously.

Day 4
Japanese cuisine.

There are four pieces of sushi, five pieces of sashimi, edamame (soybean sprouts) and a salad with ginger sauce (lightly dressed). If you want to make this dish healthier, choose a reduced sodium soy sauce and add a generous amount of fresh ginger.

Day 5

Chinese cuisine.

Various vegetables are served with steamed chicken or tofu. It's best to request that the garlic sauce is served on the side with your meal, to add about 1-30 mL of it to the dish, add 118 mL of brown rice and add another 30 mL of low-sodium soy sauce.

Day 6

Large salad entree

A variety of vegetables, topped with grilled shrimp, grilled salmon, chicken breasts, plain tuna, turkey breasts, or tofu. Chickpeas, beans, or corn will be included along with 15 mL of chopped walnuts.

Day 7

Potato and chili

Raw vegetables are unlimited in this small salad appetizer.

Raw vegetables are unlimited in this small salad appetizer. Raw vegetables are unlimited in this small salad appetizer. Additionally, one pita is made from whole wheat.

Served with a baked potato topped with low-fat sour cream and two cups of vegetarian chili.

Afternoon snack options (you must pick just one):

- Raw or fresh fruit
- 1 ounce total of nuts

- 235 mL edamame (soybeans in the pod)
- Carrot sticks and chunky salsa
- Any of the refreshments available in the morning
- Throughout the day, keep hydrating by drinking water or calorie-free flavored seltzers.

Dinner guidelines:

Pick one from each of the following categories:

Appetizers:

For the salads, use olive oil and vinegar or make a vinaigrette. Other options are a shrimp cocktail with red sauce, mussels marinara, steamed artichokes, sliced tomatoes, and veggies (mushrooms, asparagus, etc.).

Entree:

options include 5 ounces of grilled, roasted, or baked chicken breast, fish, seafood, tofu, turkey breast, lean pork (red meat once a week; however, you can have buffalo and venison more frequently), veggie burgers, turkey burgers, or soy burgers.

Unlimited vegetables:

Nothing is off-limits when it comes to vegetables. Steamed or lightly grilled with olive oil, vegetable oil, or a margarine spread containing plant sterols.

Starch:

one-half to 235 mL of starch made from whole grains; brown rice; couscous, whole-wheat pasta with olive oil or marinara sauce; or a small sweet potato.

alcohol is optional:

One glass of either red or white wine

Choices for dessert include fresh fruit, a scoop of fruit sorbet, six to eight ounces of low-fat frozen yogurt or light ice cream, or a fresh serving of fruit. In addition, you are free to consume any frozen low-fat pop beverage that has one hundred calories or fewer.

Drink a lot of sparkling water or any other variety with your dinner.

Chapter 1: Breakfast

1. HEART-HEALTHY CHOPPED POTATO BREAKFAST SALAD

INGREDIENTS

- Salad Ingredients
- 240 mL rinsed, drained canned chickpeas (garbanzo beans)
- Cut three large potatoes into ¾-inch cubes after washing and scrubbing. Approx. 720 mL

- 240 mL chopped red pepper
- Cooking spray
- Six egg whites

Dressing Ingredients

- 30 mL olive oil, extra virgin
- 30 mL of fresh lemon juice
- 240 mL fresh parsley, chopped (packed into cup measure)
- 15 mL tablespoon of real maple syrup

DIRECTIONS

Cube potatoes and enough water to cover; boil over medium heat in a large saucepan. For 5 minutes, or until soft, boil the potatoes (easily pierced with a knife). Squeeze off the excess liquid and transfer it to a serving dish.

Spray some cooking spray lightly into a nonstick skillet. Without stirring, fry the egg whites over medium heat until firm but still somewhat runny in the center. Letting the egg whites from the pan, invert it onto a cutting board. Cut up some egg whites and put them in a bowl.

Put some red pepper and chickpeas in a bowl and toss them together to blend well. Create the dressing by combining the ingredients until they are entirely smooth. Include, then gently toss the salad with the sauce.

2. LOADED QUINOA BREAKFAST BOWL

INGREDIENTS

- 60 mL unsweetened almond milk
- 59 mL tri-colored quinoa, rinsed
- 30 mL dried goji berries or dried cranberries
- 177 mL water, divided
- 30 mL vanilla extract
- 60 mL fresh or frozen unsweetened blueberries
- 15 mL of slivered almonds
- One small banana
- 15 mL of chopped walnuts
- 0.5 mL ground cinnamon
- 0.5 mL of maple syrup
- 15 mL of new pumpkin seeds

DIRECTIONS

Bring half a cup of water to a boil in a small saucepan. The addition of quinoa is essential. Cover and reduce heat to low; simmer for 12-15 minutes or until liquid is absorbed. In the meantime, soak the berries for 10 minutes in the remaining water. Slice the banana in half lengthwise. Use a knife to thinly slice one banana half and a fork to mash the other.

Take quinoa off the stove and fluff it with a fork to cool it down. Combining mashed banana, almond milk, maple syrup, Cinnamon, and vanilla is a delicious idea. Place in a bowl and top with various fruits and nuts, such as blueberries, walnuts, almonds, pumpkin seeds, banana slices, and goji berries. Add more almond milk and maple syrup to taste.

3. BANANA BLUEBERRY PANCAKES

INGREDIENTS

- 30 mL of baking powder
- 235 mL whole wheat flour
- 30 mL sugar
- 295 mL fat-free milk
- 2 mL salt
- 350 mL fresh or frozen blueberries
- One large egg, room temperature, lightly beaten
- Three medium-ripe bananas, mashed
- 5 mL of vanilla extract
- 118 mL all-purpose flour

DIRECTIONS

Mix the flour, sugar, baking powder, and salt in a large bowl. Add the wet components (egg, milk, bananas, and vanilla) to the dry ingredients and mix until combined.

Blueberries should be sprinkled on top of the batter before it is poured onto a hot skillet sprayed with cooking spray. When you see bubbles forming on top, flip it over and continue cooking until the other side is golden brown. Serve with syrup and sliced bananas, if desired.

4. NO-BAKE SUNFLOWER-OAT BARS

INGREDIENTS

- 30 mL of ground cinnamon
- 118 mL dried fruit (like raisins, blueberries, cherries, cranberries)
- 940 mL old-fashioned rolled oats (gluten-free, if needed)
- 235 mL raw sunflower seeds
- 235 mL banana chips or dried bananas, roughly chopped
- 5 mL of kosher salt
- 350 mL sunflower seed butter
- 118 mL agave nectar

DIRECTIONS

Use parchment paper to line a square 8x8-inch baking dish.

In a large bowl, mix the dry ingredients. Combine the agave nectar and sunflower seed butter by stirring them together. Pack into the dish, then chill in the fridge to set. Make bars and eat them in pieces. Don't forget to put it in the fridge! (or freezer for more extended storage).

5. SLOW COOKER OATMEAL WITH HONEY & FRUIT

INGREDIENTS

- 30 mL honey
- 2 mL salt
- 6 cups water
- 177 mL quinoa (red, white, or tri-color variety), rinsed
- 235 mL chopped dried apricots
- 177 mL steel-cut oats
- 5 mL vanilla extract (or 2 mL vanilla bean paste)
- 177 mL hazelnuts, roasted and chopped

DIRECTIONS

Pour the oats, dried apricots, vanilla, salt, honey, quinoa, and water into the bowl of a slow cooker (ideally 2 1/2 to 3 1/2 quarts in size; if yours is more extensive, you may want to consider doubling the recipe). Give it a good stir to ensure the honey gets included, and everything is well-blended.

Cover the slow cooker, turn it to its lowest setting (LOW, or 8-10 hours), and leave it on the counter overnight.

Take the top off in the morning or after waiting 8 hours, and whisk everything together again. Swirl that in if a film has developed on top of the cereal.

Put some porridge in bowls and sprinkle each with 30 mL of chopped hazelnuts. Add toppings on the side and serve.

6. BLUEBERRY MUFFINS

INGREDIENTS

- 475 mL fresh blueberries
- 5 mL of vanilla extract
- 95 mL Splenda, divided
- 118 mL unsweetened applesauce
- 5 mL cinnamon
- 60 mL egg whites (equals three egg whites)
- 240 mL 100% white whole wheat flour
- 30 mL of reduced-sodium baking powder
- 118 mL unsweetened soy milk

DIRECTIONS

Prepare a muffin tray by spraying it gently with canola oil cooking spray and baking it at 400 degrees.

Prepare a bowl of blueberries by washing, draining, and setting them aside.

Whole wheat flour, baking powder, a third of a cup of Splenda, and Cinnamon should be whisked together in a large bowl.

Egg whites should be beaten until soft peaks form in a medium bowl. Mix in the soy milk, vanilla essence, and applesauce.

Blend the dry ingredients with the egg-white mixture by folding them together. Blend in berries carefully.

Bake for 17 minutes, until the tops are light brown, then sprinkle with the remaining 15 mL of Splenda.

AVOCADO TOAST RECIPE

INGREDIENTS

- 120 mL Lemon Juice
- 1 Ripe avocado

To Taste Chilli flakes

- a good drizzle of extra virgin olive oil
- 2 Slices Sourdough bread or multigrain bread

DIRECTIONS

Carefully split the avocado in half, remove the stone, and spoon the flesh into a basin. Add the lemon juice and mash with a fork until the consistency is right.

Add salt, pepper, and sea salt to taste. hot pepper flakes

After you've toasted your bread, you may add the avocado and oil.

Get out the toaster: avocado toast is ready.

MEDITERRANEAN OMELETTE

INGREDIENTS

- Three eggs
- 30 mL olives
- 30 mL olive oil
- Salt and pepper to taste
- 30 mL white onions
- 15 mL oregano
- 15 mL spinach, blanched with butter

DIRECTIONS

The eggs should be lightly beaten with the seasonings added.

Put some oil in a pan and cook the beaten eggs in there.

Pick up a fork and gently mix the eggs.

Arrange toppings like onions, spinach, olives, and oregano, then roll up.

Repeat the folding process, and then serve.

Chapter 2: Vegetarian recipes

MINI CRUSTLESS CARAMELIZED ONION & CHEESE QUICHES

INGREDIENTS

- 60 mL chopped walnuts or pecans, toasted
- 30 mL fresh thyme leaves or finely chopped fresh parsley
- Five large eggs
- Two large sweet onions halved and sliced 1/4-inch thick
- 5 mL of kosher salt plus a pinch divided
- 15 – 60 mL water, as needed
- 235 mL finely shredded Cheddar or Gruyère cheese or crumbled goat or blue cheese
- 30 mL of avocado oil or canola oil
- 0.5 mL ground white pepper

DIRECTIONS

In a large saucepan, melt the oil over moderate heat. Put in the onions and 5 mL of salt and mix well. Cover and cook over low heat for 5 minutes. Take off the lid and mix things up. Cover and simmer until the onions have melted and turn a rich caramel color, occasionally stirring for about 35 to 45 minutes. If a fond (brown coating) forms on the bottom of the pan, deglaze it with 15 mL of water and then use a wooden spoon or spatula to scrape the fond and its flavorful bits back into the onions. After 20 minutes, remove the caramelized onions to a large bowl to cool to room temperature.

To bake successfully, heat the oven to 375 degrees Fahrenheit. Spray two mini muffin trays with enough cooking spray to fill 21 L .

In a large bowl, combine the eggs, half-and-half, pepper, and the remaining 2 mL of salt and whisk until smooth. In a medium bowl, thoroughly combine the chopped onions, grated cheese, chopped nuts (if using), and thyme (or parsley). Whisk the eggs while adding the onion mixture. Spoon the batter into the prepared muffin cups, filling them about 3/4 full (about 1 1/2 tablespoons). Stir the mixture occasionally to keep the ingredients dispersed throughout the custard.

Bake until a knife inserted in the center comes out clean, about 15 to 20 minutes, flipping the front of the pan to back and side to side halfway through baking. Mini quiches can be baked directly from the muffin tins, which should be inverted onto a baking sheet. Leave to cool for 15 minutes at room temperature on the sheet pan.

HIT THE TRAIL GRANOLA BAR

INGREDIENTS

- Cooking spray
- 60 mL low-sodium peanut butter
- 30 mL of stevia sweetener
- Stevia caramel flavored with coconut five squeezes
- 0.5 mL ground nutmeg
- Stevia sweetener flavored with coconut five squeezes
- 60 mL dry-roasted wheat germ
- 60 mL unsweetened, dried cranberries
- 1 mL ground ginger
- 235 mL puffed rice cereal
- 60 mL sliced or slivered almonds
- Two egg whites
- 5 mL of ground cinnamon
- 235 mL uncooked rolled oats

DIRECTIONS

Turn the oven temperature up to 350 degrees F. Prepare a baking dish, 8 inches on a side, by spraying it lightly with cooking spray.

A medium bowl should be filled with egg whites, stevia sweetener, peanut butter, ginger, cinnamon, and nutmeg, as well as both types of liquid stevia sweetener.

Mix in the almonds, cranberries, wheat germ, oats, and cereal. Put everything in a bowl and mix it thoroughly.

Use a spoon or dry measuring cup to press the mixture into the prepared pan. The top should be golden brown when you put it in the oven. Once cool, place on a wire rack. Once the bars have been baked, wait for at least 30 minutes before cutting them into bars.

MOROCCAN PUMPKIN & CHICKPEA STEW

INGREDIENTS

- 1-inch knob of grated ginger, or minced
- Cumin 30 mL
- Adding a pinch of red pepper flakes is a good idea
- A carrot and a potato, diced
- To taste, mineral salt and fresh cracked pepper
- Fresh baby kale or spinach (chopped or whole is fine)
- You will need 15 mL of coconut oil or olive oil, or 60 mL of water (for water saute).
- Cut two small sweet potatoes into cubes
- Approximately 700 mL - 1 L of cubed sugar pumpkin (or butternut squash)
- Coriander 30 mL
- Cinnamon stick or 5 mL of cinnamon
- Cooked chickpeas in 700 mL or two 15-ounce cans, drained and rinsed
- The amount of vegetable broth or water should be 700 mL
- Using golden raisins, I used 60 mL
- Approximately one yellow onion, diced
- Minced four garlic cloves
- Stovetop tomatoes, 830 mL
- Serving wedges of lemon or lime
- As a garnish, cilantro

DIRECTIONS

In order to prepare a pumpkin, first cut it in half lengthwise, then use a spoon to remove the seeds, and last, cut each half into four separate pieces. To remove the tough outer covering, peel the vegetable with a vegetable peeler. Alternately, you can turn the slice on its side and remove the rough peel by carefully slicing it from top to bottom. This works best if you turn the slice on its side. Cube the meat to a size of one inch.

In a large Dutch oven or pot, heat the oil over medium heat. Saute the onions for about five minutes, or until they are translucent, and then remove from the pan. Toss in the spices, garlic, and ginger, then continue to cook for one more minute, or until the mixture becomes aromatic.

Put the carrots, sweet potatoes, pumpkin, tomatoes, chickpeas, broth or water, a healthy teaspoon of salt, and the raisins in a big pot and mix everything together. Bring to a boil, then reduce heat to low, cover, and simmer for 30–40 minutes, or until the pumpkin can be easily pierced with a fork.

Put some greens in the pot, cover it, and simmer them until they become wilted, like spinach would. To enhance the flavor, season with salt, pepper, or any other seasonings of your choice, along with any other spices or even some raisins.

When ready to serve, divide the stew into individual bowls and top with rice, quinoa, or couscous, depending on personal preference. A dash of chopped cilantro and the juice of half a lemon or half a lime should be sprinkled on top. Delectable when paired with vegan naan!

To feed four to six

Extras taste even better after being refrigerated for a few days. When something is frozen, it can be stored for an additional two to three months. Put in the refrigerator to thaw for later use.

MUNG DHAL WITH SPINACH

INGREDIENTS

- 15 mL rapeseed oil
- 100 mL new potatoes, halved and boiled until tender
- 2 mL turmeric
- 5 mL chopped fresh ginger
- 150 mL mung dahl (split or husked mung beans/peas)
- 2 mL cumin seeds
- 1-2 green chilies chopped
- 250 mL spinach, washed and finely chopped
- Juice of half lime

DIRECTIONS

The dhal must be washed thoroughly with multiple changes of water.

Fry ginger, green chilis, and cumin for 1 minute in hot oil.

Cook for a further minute or so after adding the dhal and spinach.

To prepare turmeric, one and a half liters of water must be added.

Cover the pot and cook the dhal over low heat, turning regularly, until it reaches a soft consistency. More water may be required. Warm the lime juice and boiled potatoes together. Accompany with rice and pita bread.

ROAST VEGETABLE AND CHICKPEA TAGINE

INGREDIENTS

- 227 mL can of chopped tomatoes in rich natural juice
- 200–225ml hot home-made or reduced-salt vegetable stock
- Six small shallots halved
- 20 mL rapeseed oil
- 5 mL ground cumin
- 225 mL sweet potato, peeled and cut into small chunks or wedges
- Two carrots (about 225 mL total/unprepared weight), sliced
- 5 mL ground coriander
- One red pepper, deseeded and cut into chunks
- 115 mL canned chickpeas in water (drained weight), drained and rinsed
- 4–6 ready-to-eat dried apricots 25 mL, halved
- 2 mL ground cinnamon
- Chopped fresh coriander to garnish (optional)

DIRECTIONS

Set oven temperature to 200 degrees Celsius (180 degrees Celsius with the fan on) or gas. In a tiny bowl, mix the rapeseed oil and the spices.

Put the sweet potatoes, carrots, red pepper, and shallots in a medium nonstick roasting tray. Toss the vegetables with the oil mixture to combine. Vegetables should be spread out evenly, so shake the tin.

Bake at 200 degrees celsius for 25 minutes, stirring once or twice, until veggies are lightly browned and almost soft. To a roasting tin, toss in the chopped tomatoes, stock (how much you use will depend on the moisture content of the tomatoes), chickpeas, and apricots. Roast, covered, for an additional 15–20 minutes, stirring once, until bubbling and heated.

For added flavor, sprinkle with chopped coriander and serve with your choice of couscous, whole wheat bread, or baked potatoes.

SWEET POTATO BLACK BEAN CHILI

INGREDIENTS

- 120 mL of diced green chilies
- 5 mL of dried oregano
- 450 mL of black beans, drained and rinsed
- 2 – 3 garlic cloves minced
- 5 mL EACH garlic + onion powder, optional (for good measure)
- 1 1/30 mL chili powder
- One medium onion, diced
- 5 mL of pink salt, or to taste

- One large sweet potato (about one lb.), diced (with or without skin)
- 15 mL olive oil or 60 mL water (for water saute)
- 15 mL cumin
- One can (450 mL) of fire-roasted diced tomatoes (with juices) or 350 mL of chopped fresh tomatoes
- One can (180 mL) tomato paste
- 475 mL water or vegetable broth

DIRECTIONS

Saute Preheat oil in a big saucepan or Dutch oven over medium heat. After about 5-6 minutes, add the onions and sauté until they are tender and beginning to brown. Cook garlic for an additional minute. Spices (paprika, cumin, oregano, garlic, and onion) should be added and cooked for a further minute (or until fragrant).

Simmer: Add the beans, diced tomatoes, tomato paste, sweet potato, green chilies, and vegetable broth, and stir until mixed. Cook, uncovered but slightly ajar, for 30–40 minutes after coming to a boil, starting regularly. Chili is done when sweet potatoes are soft. If the chili seems too thick, add a little more water.

Garnish with whatever you choose before serving. This simple Cilantro Lime Cashew 'Sour Cream is a great addition.

Provides a delicious meal for four

Keep: Refrigerated leftovers can be stored for up to 5-6 days if stored in an airtight container. You may keep things fresher for up to two or three months if you freeze them in freezer-safe containers.

ONE-POT LENTIL & VEGETABLE SOUP WITH PARMESAN

INGREDIENTS

- 30 mL extra-virgin olive oil
- 350 mL green or brown lentils
- 940 mL low-sodium vegetable or chicken broth
- 1 mL crushed red pepper
- Parmesan rind (optional)
- 700 mL packed roughly chopped lacinato kale
- 450 mL can of unsalted diced tomatoes, undrained
- 30 mL of finely chopped fresh thyme
- 700 mL fresh or frozen chopped onion, carrot and celery mix
- Four cloves garlic, chopped
- 22 mL red wine vinegar
- Chopped fresh flat-leaf parsley for garnish
- 80 mL grated Parmesan cheese
- 1 mL salt
- 1 mL ground pepper

DIRECTIONS

Prepare the oil in a big saucepan or Dutch oven by heating it over medium heat. Cook the carrot, celery, and onion mixture for 6-10 minutes, stirring, until it has softened. Stirring often, sauté the garlic for about 30 seconds or until the aroma has mellowed.

Combine the lentils, tomatoes, thyme, salt, pepper, crushed red pepper, and Parmesan rind (if using) in a large pot and simmer for 30 minutes. Cook at a steady boil for about five minutes. Add water as needed to get the desired consistency; simmer, covered, for 15–25 minutes or until lentils are almost tender.

Blend in the kale. Kale should be cooked for around 5-10 minutes with the lid on. If using Parmesan cheese, peel off the rind and throw it away. Add vinegar and mix well. Dish out the soup into six bowls and top each serving with a generous helping of Parmesan. Sprinkle some chopped parsley on top if using.

ROASTED ROOT VEGGIES & GREENS OVER SPICED LENTILS

INGREDIENTS

- 350 mL water
- 1 mL ground allspice
- One clove of garlic smashed
- 350 mL roasted root vegetables (see associated recipes)
- 475 mL chopped kale or beet greens
- 1 mL ground cumin
- 30 mL of lemon juice
- 5 mL of extra-virgin olive oil
- 15 mL of extra-virgin olive oil
- 5 mL of ground coriander
- 0.5 mL ground pepper
- Pinch of kosher salt
- 30 mL tahini or low-fat plain yogurt
- 1 mL kosher salt
- 80 mL black beluga lentils or French green lentils
- 5 mL of garlic powder
- 1 mL ground coriander
- Fresh parsley for garnish

DIRECTIONS

Lentils need to be prepared in the following ways: In a medium saucepan, mix the water, lentils, garlic powder, 2 mL of ground coriander, cumin, allspice, 1 mL of salt, and sumac (if using). Raise the temperature until it boils. Cover, keep at a simmer, and cook for 25-30 minutes or until tender.

Remove the lid and cook for another 5 minutes or until the liquid has reduced significantly. Drain. Mix in 5 mL of oil and lemon juice.

In the meantime, prepare the vegetables: Prepare a big skillet with oil and heat it over medium heat. The flavor will begin to emerge one to two minutes after adding the garlic. Toss in the roasted root vegetables and simmer for 2 to 4 minutes, frequently turning, until warm. Toss in the kale (or beet greens) and simmer for 2 to 3 minutes or until wilted. Coriander, pepper, and salt should be stirred in.

Prepare the lentils as usual, and then top them with the vegetables and tahini (or yogurt). Sprinkle some chopped parsley on top if using.

Chapter 3: Meat and Poultry

1.ROSEMARY LAMB SHISH KABOBS

INGREDIENTS

- 1 mL dried oregano
- 1 mL dried thyme
- ½ lemon, grated rind and juice
- One 450 mL lean lamb
- 60 mL of olive oil
- One red bell pepper, deseeded
- One garlic clove, crushed
- rosemary sprigs, a bundle of 6-8" long stems
- Two onions

DIRECTIONS

Lamb should be cleaned of extra fat and sliced into large, uniform cubes measuring about an inch on a side.

Get a hold of one of the onions and carefully grate or chop it. Then, squeeze the chopped onion over a big glass bowl to collect the juice. Toss the onion juice with olive oil, lemon juice, crushed garlic, oregano, and thyme. Marinate the lamb for at least two hours, preferably overnight, by adding the meat to the liquid and putting it in the fridge.

Cut the second onion in half or into wedges. Peel and chop the red bell pepper. Take the lamb out of the marinade and set the marinade aside to use later as a basting sauce. Starting at the bottom of the rosemary sprigs' stems, thread the meat onto them. Swap out the red bell pepper and onion slices.

The extra rosemary leaves can be crushed and sprinkled on the lamb as a seasoning.

Cook for 8 to 10 minutes on the grill, basting and regularly flipping with the marinade you saved. Start serving right away. Serves 4–6.

Serve over saffron rice for a delicious main course.

2. BEEFY SWEET & SLOPPY JOES

INGREDIENTS

- 30 mL Ground Beef
- 15 mL of Worcestershire sauce
- One medium yellow bell pepper
- 177 mL white onion
- 30 mL brown sugar
- One can 350 mL vegetable juice
- Four each whole-wheat hamburger buns

DIRECTIONS

Bring to temperature a big, nonstick skillet over moderate heat. Cook the ground beef, bell pepper, and onion for 8 to 10 minutes while breaking it up into 3/4-inch chunks and stirring regularly.

Add vegetable juice, brown sugar, and Worcestershire sauce to a pot and boil. Simmer, uncovered, on low heat for 7 to 9 minutes, occasionally stirring, until most of the liquid has evaporated and a minor thickening has occurred.

Spread the beef mixture evenly over the bottom halves of the buns, then close the sandwiches.

3. TOP SIRLOIN STEAK, GREEN BEAN AND TOMATO SALAD

INGREDIENTS

- 30 mL Top Sirloin Steak
- 940 mL fresh baby spinach
- 60 mL Parmesan cheese
- 60 mL plus 30 mL of balsamic vinaigrette
- 235 mL grape tomatoes
- 2-1/475 mL green beans
- 5 mL of olive oil

DIRECTIONS

Split the beef steak in half lengthwise, then slice it crosswise into thin strips (about 1/8 to 1/4 inch thick). Mix 30 mL of dressing with the meat in a medium bowl. Marinate for 30 minutes to 2 hours, covered, in the fridge.

A big, nonstick skillet should be heated over medium heat until hot. Stir-fry green beans with a teaspoon of oil for 5 minutes. Stir in the tomatoes and cook for another 2–3 minutes, or until the beans are crisp-tender and the tomatoes have begun to color. Take out of pan and season to taste with salt and pepper. It would help if you kept warm.

Half of the beef should be added to the same pan and stir-fried for another 1-3 minutes or until the exterior is no longer pink. Take out of the skillet. Again, with the remaining beef.

To serve, divide the spinach across four dishes. Sprinkle with seasoning and serve with beef and vegetables. Spread some cheese on top. Using the remaining 60 mL of dressing, drizzle the salad.

4. TANGY LIME GRILLED TOP ROUND STEAK

INGREDIENTS

- honeydew
- 60 mL fresh lime juice
- 30 mL of vegetable oil
- 15 mL of Worcestershire sauce
- 1 Top Round Steak
- Three large garlic
- 30 mL brown sugar

DIRECTIONS

Mix the juice, sugar, oil, Worcestershire, and garlic in a small bowl. Coat the beef steak with the lime mixture by placing it in a plastic bag and turning it over. Marinate in the fridge for at least 6 hours, preferably overnight, and rotate the bag occasionally.

Take the steak out of the marinade and throw it away. The best steaks are grilled over a medium bed of ash. For a medium rare (145°F) doneness, grill, covered, for 10 to 11 minutes (over medium heat on a preheated gas grill, durations remain the same). (Avoid cooking to mush!)

Prepare steak by slicing it thinly. If you like salt and pepper, add some.

5.BEEFY SWEET POTATO MASH-UP

INGREDIENTS

- One large sweet potatoes
- 475 mL yellow onion
- 30 mL Ground Beef
- 15 mL of vegetable oil
- 60 mL Greek-style yogurt
- 20 mL of taco seasoning mix
- 2 mL hot pepper sauce
- 118 mL water

- One large sweet potatoes
- 1-1/475 mL yellow onion
- 30 mL Ground Beef
- 15 mL of vegetable oil
- 60 mL Greek-style yogurt
- 20 mL of taco seasoning mix
- 30 mL of fresh cilantro
- Eight small corn tortillas

DIRECTIONS

Bring to temperature a big, nonstick skillet over moderate heat. In a large skillet, brown ground beef over medium heat for 8 to 10 minutes, breaking it into 1/2-inch crumbles with a wooden spoon. It's essential to clean up any spills. Add a quarter cup of water and 30 mL of taco seasoning and stir; simmer for 3 minutes. Get it out of the pan and keep it warm.

In the same pan, toss the sweet potatoes, the onions, the remaining 60 mL of water, and the other 30 mL of taco seasoning. Start a pot of water boiling. Simmer, covered, for 10 minutes, stirring once. Take off the lid, add the oil, and keep cooking uncovered for another 4 to 6 minutes, occasionally stirring, until the potatoes are soft and beginning to brown. Cook the meat mixture for 2 to 4 minutes, stirring periodically until cooked.

In the meantime, in a separate small bowl, mix the yogurt and the spicy sauce.

Distribute the beef filling evenly among the tortillas. Serve with yogurt sauce and cilantro on the side if you want.

6. TRADITIONAL BEEF TENDERLOIN ROAST WITH A DRIZZLE OF CRANBERRY SAUCE

INGREDIENTS

- 4 mL yellow onions, peeled, cut into wedges
- 595 mL Brussels sprouts, trimmed
- 15 mL pepper

- One beef Tenderloin Roast Center-Cut (2 to 3 pounds)
- 15 mL of olive oil
- 6 mL salt, divided
- 30 mL chopped fresh thyme leaves

DIRECTIONS

Preheat oven to 425 degrees Fahrenheit. Mix the onions, Brussels sprouts, oil, and 5 mL of salt on a metal baking sheet. I am putting aside.

To save time in the kitchen, use Cipollini or pearl onions instead of yellow onions after they have been peeled and sliced into thin rounds instead of wedges. Cipollini onions are grape hyacinth bulbs that look and taste like little, flat onions. Wild onions are a popular item in the fresh produce sections of many major supermarkets. You only need 10 to 15 seconds in boiling water to make peeling a breeze. Take it out of the pot and put it straight into the icy water. Prepare a draining solution and peel the skin.

In a small bowl, mix the thyme and the pepper. Remove 5 mL of the thyme mixture and keep it aside for the sauce. Apply the leftover thyme mixture to the steak by pressing it into the meat in an even layer. Roast Tenderloin.

Rack a roast and put it in a shallow roasting pan. Put the probe of an oven-safe meat thermometer right in the middle of the beef's thickest area. Keep the lid off, and don't add any water. Cook the vegetables alongside the roast. Beef roasting at 425 degrees Medium-rare meat should be cooked for 35–45 minutes, whereas medium-done beef should be cooked for 45–50 minutes. In a preheated oven, roast veggies for 45–50 minutes or until soft and just beginning to brown.

7.KOREAN CHICKEN TACOS

INGREDIENTS

- One 60 mL kimchi
- 15 mL of lime juice
- 30 mL of packed brown sugar
- 90 mL of reduced-sodium soy sauce
- 15 mL of vegetable oil
- 1 ½ pound skinless, boneless chicken breast halves cut into bite-size strips
- 7 mL grated fresh ginger
- Two cloves garlic, minced
- 8 5-6 inch white corn tortillas, heated according to package directions
- 5 mL of Asian chili-garlic sauce
- 5 mL cornstarch

DIRECTIONS

Whisk together the soy sauce, lime juice, brown sugar, ginger, garlic, cornstarch, and chili-garlic sauce in a small bowl.

Oil should be heated over medium heat in a big skillet. Then, add the chicken and cook and stir it for about 8-10 minutes, or until the meat is no longer pink. Combine soy sauce and water, then stir it into the chicken in the pan. Keep cooking and going until the mixture thickens and bubbles.

Wrap the warm tortillas around the chicken mixture and kimchi. Scatter some chopped cilantro on top, and if you like, some Korean barbecue sauce.

8. PRESSURE-COOKER ZITI WITH ITALIAN CHICKEN SAUSAGE

INGREDIENTS

- 30 mL Italian seasoning, crushed
- 240 mL dried ziti or bow-tie pasta
- 80 mL chopped fresh basil
- 235 mL shredded provolone or mozzarella cheese
- 12 ounces of completely cooked chicken sausage made in the Italian way, cut in half lengthwise and sliced
- One 240 mL can of tomato sauce
- Four cloves garlic, minced
- 80 mL chicken broth

DIRECTIONS

Combine the first seven ingredients in a 6-quart electric or stovetop pressure cooker (with Italian seasoning). Use the saute function on an electric range to get water boiling. Put everything right into the saucepan when using a stovetop oven. Reduce heat and simmer, uncovered, for 5 minutes. Add spaghetti and mix well. Secure the top. For 8 minutes of high-pressure cooking, set your electric cooker. Over medium-high heat, bring a stovetop pressure cooker to pressure, then turn down the heat just enough to keep the pressure stable without making it too high. Put something in the oven for 8 minutes. Take it away from the stove. Wait 15 minutes for the pressure to relax naturally in both models. The residual tension must be released. Gently lift the container's lid.

Add basil and mix gently. Bake with cheese on top. Cover the cheese and let it sit out for 5 minutes if you want it to melt.

9.CORNBREAD CHICKEN WITH KALE

INGREDIENTS

- 6 cups coarsely chopped kale
- 177 mL cornbread stuffing mix, crushed
- Two 240 mL skinless, boneless chicken breast halves, cut in half horizontally
- Nonstick cooking spray
- 60 mL balsamic vinegar
- 1 mL salt
- 30 mL of olive oil
- 80 mL thinly sliced onion (1 medium)
- 1 mL ground black pepper

DIRECTIONS

Turn on the oven to 250F. Spread the stuffing mix out on a pie plate. Spray cooking spray lightly over the chicken. Cover the chicken in the stuffing mixture by dipping it and turning it over.

15 mL of the oil, extra big skillet, medium heat. Add chicken; cook, rotating once, for 6 to 8 minutes, or until chicken is no longer pink (165°F) and the coating is golden. After turning the chicken, you may need to add extra oil to the pan. Put chicken on a baking pan and into the oven to stay warm.

Disinfect the pan. Put the onion in the pan with the remaining tablespoon of oil. Keep stirring for another 3–4 minutes or until the onion is soft. Toss in the kale, vinegar, salt, pepper, and stir-fry until the kale wilts. Prepare a kale-chicken combination and serve.

10. MARINATED CHICKEN BREASTS

INGREDIENTS

- 1 to 30 mL mustard, whole grain or Dijon
- 60 mL extra-virgin olive oil
- Kosher salt and freshly ground black pepper
- 1 to 30 mL vinegar, like cider, balsamic, or red wine
- Four boneless, skinless chicken breasts, each about 6 ounces
- 10 mL to 15 mL of dried herbs, like thyme, oregano, rosemary, or crumbled bay leaf

DIRECTIONS

Put all the ingredients (vinegar, herbs, mustard, powders (if using), and oil) into a large resealable plastic bag and shake well. Put a lid on the bag and shake it up to mix the contents. The chicken breast should be placed into the opened bag. If you want an even coating, seal the bag and shake it. Please put it in the freezer for up to two weeks.

You can let it thaw in the fridge overnight, pour cold water over it, or zap it in the microwave at 30% power for 1 minute.

Prepare a grill or pan for grilling. Place the chicken on the grill once it is hot, and cook for about 4 minutes per side or until cooked through. The chicken can be baked in an oven at 375 degrees F for 15 minutes or until cooked.

Chapter 4: Fish and Seafoods

MEDITERRANEAN SOLE

INGREDIENTS

- 30 mL dry white wine or chicken broth
- 450 mL sole fillets, cut into four portions
- 1 mL pepper
- One medium lemon, sliced
- 475 mL cherry tomatoes, halved
- 118 mL Greek olives, halved
- 15 mL of capers, drained
- 15 mL of lemon juice
- Two garlic cloves minced
- 30 mL olive oil divided
- 30 mL minced fresh parsley

DIRECTIONS

Fire up the oven to 400 degrees. Spread each fillet on a sheet of sturdy foil or paper (about 12 in. square). Pepper the fillets and lay slices of lemon on top. Add a splash of wine and a teaspoon of oil, and stir.

Spread fillets with a mixture of tomato, olive, caper, lemon juice, garlic, and a tablespoon of oil. Wrap fish tightly in foil or parchment paper.

Prepare a baking sheet for the packets. Ten to twelve minutes in the oven should be enough time for the fish to start flaking. Carefully rip open packages to release steam. Add some chopped parsley.

GRILLED MAHI MAHI

INGREDIENTS

- Eight Mahi Mahi fillets (180 mL each)
- 177 mL reduced-sodium teriyaki sauce
- Two garlic cloves
- 30 mL of sherry or pineapple juice

Tropical fruit salsa:

- 118 mL cubed fresh pineapple
- 1/2 medium red onion, chopped
- 2 mL crushed red pepper flakes
- 15 mL of lime juice
- 15 mL of lemon juice
- 60 mL minced fresh cilantro
- One medium mango, peeled and diced
- 60 mL minced fresh mint
- 15 mL chopped seeded jalapeno pepper
- 177 mL chopped green pepper
- 235 mL chopped, seeded, peeled papaya

DIRECTIONS

Mix the teriyaki sauce, sherry, and garlic in a shallow dish, then add the Mahi-mahi. To coat, toss; then, cover and chill for 30 minutes.

In the meantime, mix all the salsa ingredients in a big bowl. Keep covered and chilled until ready to serve.

The fillets should be drained of the marinade and thrown away. Grill the Mahi Mahi over a rack that has been greased. Cook covered fish over medium heat for 4 to 5 minutes per side, or broil 4 inches from the heat. Toss with salsa and serve.

PAN-SEARED SALMON WITH DILL SAUCE

INGREDIENTS

- 118 mL reduced-fat plain yogurt
- Four salmon fillets (180 mL each)
- 1 mL salt
- 60 mL finely chopped cucumber
- 5 mL of Italian seasoning
- 15 mL of canola oil
- 60 mL reduced-fat mayonnaise
- 5 mL of snipped fresh dill

DIRECTIONS

Oil should be heated over medium heat in a big skillet. Season the salmon with the salt and Italian spice on hand. Cook with the skin side down in a skillet. Turn the temperature down to medium-low. Fish should be cooked for about 5 minutes per side or until it flakes easily with a fork.

While that's going on, mix some yogurt, mayonnaise, cucumber, and dill in a separate bowl. Prepare alongside salmon.

SESAME-CRUSTED TUNA WITH ASIAN SLAW

INGREDIENTS

- 30 mL chopped sweet onion
- One small sweet red pepper, julienned
- One medium Granny Smith apple, julienned
- One medium pear, peeled and julienned
- 118 mL julienned carrot
- One package (300 mL) of shredded red cabbage (about 1 L)
- 1 mL salt
- 235 mL sesame ginger salad dressing, divided
- 118 mL sesame seeds
- Four tuna steaks (180 mL each)

DIRECTIONS

Mix the first six in a big bowl. Mix in a quarter cup of dressing and some salt and toss.

Separately, put the remaining 177 mL of dressing and the sesame seeds in small bowls. Coat both sides of the tuna with the sauce, then roll it in the sesame seeds.

Cook the tuna for two to three minutes per side over medium heat in a large skillet until medium rare—Combo well with slaw.

CITRUS SALMON EN PAPILLOTE

INGREDIENTS

- Six orange slices
- 30 mL minced fresh parsley
- 30 mL fresh asparagus, trimmed and halved
- Six lime slices
- Olive oil-flavored cooking spray
- 2 mL salt
- Six salmon fillets (120 mL each)
- 1 mL pepper
- 90 mL of lemon juice

DIRECTIONS

Have a temperature of 425 degrees in the oven ready. Fold in half six pieces of parchment paper or heavy-duty foil 15 inches by 10 inches. Spread the citrus slices out on one side of each piece. Mix up some fish and asparagus for flavor. Coat with cooking spray. Add salt, pepper, and parsley and stir to combine. Sprinkle with freshly squeezed lemon juice.

Draw the edges of the parchment together, then crimp them shut with your fingers to make a secure pouch for the fish. Put in tins for the oven.

Bake for 12-15 minutes or until fish flakes readily when tested with a fork. Carefully rip open packages to release steam.

HEART-HEALTHY FISH THAT'S PERFECT FOR A LIGHT DINNER

INGREDIENTS

- Salt and pepper
- 30 mL of low-sodium soy sauce or coconut aminos
- Oil for the pan
- Fresh parsley and orange zest for garnish
- Two cloves garlic, minced
- 60 mL orange juice
- 15 mL honey
- 12 ounces salmon, cut into 90 mL to 120 mL fillets of equal size

DIRECTIONS

Combine the honey, garlic, orange juice, and soy/coconut aminos in a bowl.

In a heated skillet, heat enough oil to coat the bottom.

Salt and pepper the salmon, then cook it skin-side down for about 5 minutes.

After being flipped, the salmon needs an extra 3–5 minutes of cooking time.

After 2 minutes, turn the salmon over, so the skin side is down and pour the sauce over it.

Apply the sauce like a glaze over the tops of the salmon fillets, and then take them from the stove.

Season with salt and pepper and, if you like, garnish with fresh parsley and orange zest.

AIR FRYER TUNA STEAK TOSTADAS WITH JICAMA SLAW

INGREDIENTS

- 30 mL of fresh lime juice
- 5 mL of ground cumin
- 475 mL peeled and diced jicama (about one small)
- 30 mL of olive oil
- 5 mL chili powder and 5 mL chili powder, divided use
- Eight 6-inch corn tortillas
- One medium mango, diced
- 15 mL plus 5 mL of honey
- Four tuna steaks (about 120 mL each)
- Cooking spray
- 475 mL shredded red cabbage (about 1/2 small head)
- Two medium limes, cut into four wedges each

DIRECTIONS

Combine the lime juice, oil, 5 mL of chili powder, and the cumin in a large glass serving dish and mix well. Toss in the fish, then turn to coat. Please put it in the fridge for 15 minutes to an hour, cover it, and turn it over a few times. Fish should be drained, and the marinade should be thrown away.

Start preheating the air fryer to 380 degrees Fahrenheit once the fish has finished marinating. Spread the fish out evenly in the air fryer basket. (Do not crowd; divide into smaller groups as necessary.) Prepare as desired by cooking for 3–4 minutes per side. Tend to the fish for 5 minutes. Slice thinly against the grain.

While that is happening, crank the oven temperature to 400 degrees Fahrenheit. The tortillas should be lightly sprayed with cooking spray. Tortillas, cooked in batches for 3 minutes on each side, will be crisp and golden.

Put the ingredients on each tortilla in the following sequence to make the tostadas: Mix the mango, fish, and 14 of the cabbage and jicama. Add half a teaspoon of honey to each. Put one lime wedge on each and squeeze. Add the remaining chili powder, about 1/8 teaspoon, to each serving. Put some cilantro on top. Quickly dish it up.

VIETNAMESE BROILED COD WITH ASPARAGUS, PEAS, AND WATER CHESTNUT STIR-FRY

INGREDIENTS

- 15 mL canola or corn oil and 15 mL canola or corn oil, divided use
- One 2-inch piece of ginger root, peeled and coarsely chopped
- Two medium garlic cloves
- Four firm white fish fillets (about 180 mL each), such as cod, halibut, or sea bass, rinsed and patted dry
- 30 mL oyster sauce (lowest sodium available)
- 30 mL water and 1 to 30 mL water, divided use
- Four medium green onions, chopped, green and white parts separated
- One bunch of medium asparagus spears, trimmed and cut into 2-inch pieces
- Two 240 mL cans of sliced water chestnuts, rinsed and drained
- 15 mL of brown sugar
- One 385 mL bag of frozen peas, thawed and drained

DIRECTIONS

Puree the white sections of the green onions with the oyster sauce, 30 mL of water, the brown sugar, 15 mL of oil, the gingerroot, and the garlic for 1 minute in a food processor or blender. Set aside 30 mL of the mixture. Keep it covered and chilled.

A shallow dish is ideal for the fish. Cover the fish in the remaining marinade and turn to coat. Keep covered and chill for 1-12 hours, rotating occasionally.

Prepare the oven or broiler for cooking when ready. Aluminum foil is used to line a baking pan.

Fish should be drained, and the marinade should be thrown away. If any marinade is left on the fish, blot it out with paper towels.

For 10 minutes, with the broiler door ajar, broil the fish at a distance of 4 to 6 inches from the heat source or until it flakes readily when probed with a fork.

In the meantime, heat the remaining 15 mL of oil in a large nonstick skillet or wok over high heat, stirring to coat the bottom.

Cook the asparagus for 3 minutes, until almost tender, stirring constantly. Stir in the water chestnuts, peas, 30 mL reserved marinade, and the remaining 15 mL water. Cook for 3 to 4 minutes or until the peas are cooked, stirring constantly. (Add 15 mL of water if the marinade looks like it might begin to burn while cooking.) Remove from the heat. Serve the vegetable stir-fry with the fish.

Chapter 5: Sides and Soups

HEART-HEALTHY MIXED BEAN SALAD RECIPE

INGREDIENTS

- 45 mL Extra virgin olive oil
- 60 mL Red onion, chopped
- 540 ml Bean Salad mix, rinsed and strained
- 3 Garlic cloves pressed
- 30 mL White wine vinegar
- 15 mL Dijon mustard
- 5 mL Honey
- 2 mL Salt and pepper
- 118 mL Cilantro, chopped

DIRECTIONS

Extract the liquid from the beans by rinsing them.

Put the drained beans, onions, and cilantro in a salad bowl. Beans, chopped cilantro, and minced red onion are featured up close in a white bowl set against a white wooden background.

Honey, salt, pepper, vinegar, mustard, olive oil, and garlic should be mixed in a small bowl. Dressing for a mixed bean salad, including garlic, olive oil, dijon mustard, honey, and white wine vinegar, whisked together in a close-up of a white bowl.

Toss the beans with the dressing.

HEART HEALTHY SOUP RECIPE

INGREDIENTS

- Eight large cloves of garlic crushed
- 1 L and 500 mL low-sodium beef broth
- 900 mL 95% lean ground beef
- One medium onion chopped
- 420 mL can of no-salt-added diced tomatoes
- 30 mL extra-virgin olive oil
- 30 mL green beans cut into 1-inch pieces
- 30 mL Worcestershire sauce
- 2 mL black pepper
- 8 mL red wine vinegar
- Fresh minced parsley for garnish
- 30 mL of dried Italian herb seasoning
- Four large stalks of celery chopped
- Four large carrots chopped
- 445 mL can of no-salt-added tomato sauce

DIRECTIONS

Put the oil in a 5-quart pot and heat it over medium. In a large skillet, brown the beef with the onion, celery, carrot, and garlic for 7 to 10 minutes while stirring regularly.

Mix the green beans, Worcestershire, Italian herb spice, seasoning, black pepper, and beef broth. Bring to a boil, then reduce heat to a simmer, cover, and cook for 15 to 20 minutes, stirring periodically, until the veggies are cooked.

Remove from heat and add vinegar, stirring to combine. If more salt is needed, taste it.

Fresh parsley is optional as a garnish for the soup.

GLUTEN-FREE PEAR AND APPLE SALADS WITH GOAT CHEESE AND ALMONDS

INGREDIENTS

- 5 mL of olive oil
- One apple, cored and thinly sliced
- 1 mL vanilla
- 0.5 mL pepper
- Two firm-ripe pears, cored and thinly sliced
- 15 mL chèvre (goat) cheese, crumbled
- 15 mL of sliced almonds, toasted
- 7 mL honey
- 15 mL of lemon juice
- 235 mL spinach leaves, torn into bite-size pieces

DIRECTIONS

In a large bowl, beat lemon juice, honey, oil, vanilla and pepper with a whisk. Add pears, apple and spinach; toss to coat.

Divide the mixture among four serving plates. Top with almonds and cheese.

MUSTARD AND HONEY CAULIFLOWER MEDLEY

INGREDIENTS

- 475 mL ready-to-eat baby-cut carrots
- Four medium green onions, cut into 1/4-inch pieces
- 15 mL of Dijon mustard
- 940 mL fresh cauliflower florets
- 30 mL honey
- 1 mL salt
- 60 mL water
- 1 mL dried or 2 mL fresh thyme leaves

DIRECTIONS

Put the oil in a 5-quart pot and heat it over medium. In a large skillet, brown the beef with the onion, celery, carrot, and garlic for 7 to 10 minutes while stirring regularly.

Mix the green beans, Worcestershire, Italian herb spice, seasoning, black pepper, and beef broth. Bring to a boil, then reduce heat to a simmer, cover, and cook for 15 to 20 minutes, stirring periodically, until the veggies are cooked.

Remove from heat and add vinegar, stirring to combine. If more salt is needed, taste it.

Fresh parsley is optional as a garnish for the soup.

CARLA'S SORGHUM WITH BUTTERNUT SQUASH

INGREDIENTS

- 235 mL uncooked sorghum
- 1 mL kosher salt
- Two garlic cloves minced
- 1 mL ground black pepper
- 80 mL finely diced onion
- 80 mL finely diced or sliced celery
- 5 mL of chopped fresh thyme leaves
- 30 mL of red wine vinegar
- 1 mL kosher salt
- 475 mL finely diced or sliced butternut squash
- 30 mL extra-virgin olive oil
- 60 mL finely chopped fresh Italian parsley
- 30 mL pumpkin seeds, toasted

DIRECTIONS

Sorghum should be cooked per the package's directions.

Oil should be heated over medium heat in a wide, flat-bottomed skillet. Mix in the onion, celery, garlic, 2 mL salt, and 1 mL of pepper—two minutes of cooking time, with constant stirring. Cook the squash for 6 minutes, tossing it around occasionally. Cook for another 3 minutes, stirring periodically until the vegetables are soft. Cook for about a minute after adding the vinegar, often stirring, until the liquid has completely evaporated.

Combine half a teaspoon of salt with the sorghum. Incorporate all heat by stirring. Remove from heat and stir in the parsley. Place in a serving dish and sprinkle with pumpkin seeds before serving. Prepare and operate at a temperature of your choosing (hot, warm, or room temperature).

BROCCOLINI WITH PEAS & SEARED LEMONS

INGREDIENTS

- 1 mL coarse salt
- 240 mL Swiss chard, trimmed and cut into 2- to 3-inch lengths
- 235 mL frozen peas
- 30 mL butter
- One lemon, thinly sliced
- 900 mL Broccolini, trimmed
- 1 mL crushed red pepper
- 60 mL chives
- 60 mL chicken broth

DIRECTIONS

Start by boiling 6-8 cups of salted water. After 2 minutes, add the broccoli florets, the Swiss chard and the peas. Cover and simmer for 4 minutes or until the green has brightened. Drain. In the meantime, heat the butter in a deep skillet. When the butter has browned, add the lemon slices for about 3 minutes on each side and continue cooking over medium heat until the lemons are tender and caramelized. (Avoid jostling them too much to obtain a good sear on the lemons.) Drain the broccoli, Swiss chard, and peas, and put them back in the pot. Toss the pan contents with the broth and smashed red pepper. Place the broccoli medley and lemons on a serving plate. To serve, sprinkle some chives and coarse salt on top.

FENNEL AND ORANGE SALAD

INGREDIENTS

- 60 mL olive oil
- Butterhead (Bibb or Boston) lettuce leaves
- Two medium blood oranges
- Two medium fennel bulbs
- 30 mL of balsamic vinegar
- Snipped fresh chives

DIRECTIONS

Fennel bulbs should have their tops trimmed and thrown away; you can save some feathery leaves if you choose. The bottoms of the fennel bulbs should be sliced thinly. Strip off and throw away any wilted outer layers. Slice the fennel bulbs into thin rounds, about 1/4 inch thick, and throw away the cores. put aside

Blood oranges should be peeled and sectioned over a large bowl to catch the juice. Dressing can be made by combining the reserved orange juice,* olive oil, and vinegar in the same bowl.

Lay lettuce leaves on four salad plates. Lay out the fennel and orange parts on a bed of lettuce and top with chives—salads with dressing. Reserved fennel leaves can be used as a garnish for salads—a side dish for four people.

ASIAN GREEN BEANS WITH WILD MUSHROOMS AND CIPOLLINI ONIONS

INGREDIENTS

- 80 mL sodium-reduced vegetable or chicken stock
- 900 mL green beans, trimmed
- 15 mL sodium-reduced tamari or sodium-reduced soy sauce
- 10 mL vegetable oil
- 450 mL Cipollini onions
- 15 mL sesame oil
- 0.5 mL pepper
- 225 mL wild mushrooms, sliced

DIRECTIONS

Put the mushrooms and oil in a large skillet and cook over medium heat until they release their water, about 8 minutes.

Remove the outer layer of onion skin and cut it in half lengthwise. Toss in the mushrooms and cook over low heat, occasionally turning, for about 10 minutes or until the mushrooms are soft and caramelized.

Cover and simmer over low heat for 15 more minutes, or until soft, after adding the stock.

Meanwhile, cook the green beans in either boiling water or a microwave for about three minutes or until they are tender but still bright green. Drain and add to the drained onion and mushroom combination along with the tamari, sesame oil, salt, and pepper.

Chapter 6: Desserts

CRANBERRY CRUMBLE BARS

INGREDIENTS

For the Filling:

- 22 mL cornstarch
- 475 mL cranberries
- Zest and juice of ½ orange
- Six tablespoons of granulated sugar
- 30 mL of almond extract
- 1 mL ground cinnamon

For the Crust:

- 350 mL all-purpose flour
- 1 mL salt
- Two large egg whites
- 350 mL almond flour
- 80 mL granulated sugar
- 5 mL of baking powder
- 1 mL ground nutmeg
- Zest of ½ orange
- 60 mL cold unsalted butter, cubed
- 7 mL vanilla extract

DIRECTIONS

Have a 375-degree Fahrenheit oven ready. Prepare a 9-by-13-inch baking dish by lining it with parchment paper and leaving an overhang on the long edges. (That further weight will come in handy when removing the bars.)

Filling prep entails: In a small dish, mix the cranberries, orange zest, orange juice, six tablespoons of granulated sugar, cornstarch, almond essence, and Cinnamon. I am putting aside.

The steps for making crust are as follows. In a giant bowl, combine the all-purpose flour, almond flour, 118 mL granulated sugar, baking powder, salt, nutmeg, and orange zest and whisk until combined. Use your hands to press and rub the butter into the mixture until it resembles coarse sand and the particles have flattened.

Use a fork to gently combine the egg whites and vanilla extract in a tiny bowl. Pour the egg whites into the flour mixture and use a knife to fold them from the edges and the middle. Do this until the egg whites are thoroughly mixed. Save half a cup of the mixture.

The remaining dough can be pressed into the bottom of the prepared baking dish.

When ready to assemble and bake, give the cranberry mixture a quick swirl before pouring it evenly over the crust. Top with the crust mixture you set aside earlier.

For about 40 minutes, or until the top is lightly browned. After 15 minutes, remove the bars from the oven and place them on a wire rack. Carefully peel the parchment off using the long edges and set it down on a cutting board. Prepare 15 pieces by slicing the bar with a knife. Requires an entire cooling-down period. If you'd like, sprinkle some powdered sugar on top before serving.

PEACH BREAD PUDDING WITH BOURBON SAUCE

INGREDIENTS

- 60 mL to 80 mL cup sugar (depending on the sweetness of the peaches)
- 595 mL frozen unsweetened sliced peaches, thawed
- Cooking spray
- Two large eggs
- Eight 1/2-inch slices of baguette-style French bread (preferably day-old)
- 235 mL fat-free milk
- 30 mL light tub margarine (softened)
- 2 mL ground cinnamon
- Three medium fresh peaches, peeled and sliced
- 30 mL dried unsweetened cherries or blueberries, or raisins (optional)

DIRECTIONS

Fat-free milk, 240 mL

1/2 of a fat-free, sugar-free vanilla 0.240 mL package packaged, ready-to-use pudding mix (approximately 67 mL).

1 mL of rum extract or 15 mL of bourbon or rum

SNICKERDOODLE COOKIES

INGREDIENTS

- 5 mL vanilla extract
- 475 mL all-purpose flour
- One egg
- 5 mL baking powder
- 60 mL stevia sugar blend (Truvia) or 80 mL cane sugar
- 5 mL cinnamon
- 2 mL salt
- 235 mL vegetable margarine or vegan butter — free from trans fats

DIRECTIONS

Preheating the oven to 400 degrees Fahrenheit (204 degrees Celsius)

Use a hand, stand, or electric mixer to cream the butter and sugar together. The recipe calls for 15 mL of sugar, so set that aside.

Add the egg and vanilla once the batter has become frothy.

Stir the flour, baking soda, and salt in a separate dish.

Add the dry ingredients to the wet and stir between each addition. Avoid a disaster by not over-blending.

The Cinnamon and the sugar you set aside should be mixed in a separate basin.

Roll the dough into balls about an inch in diameter, and then coat the balls in the sugar. Spread them on a baking sheet and gently press down on each one with a fork or spoon.

Put in oven and set a timer for 8-10 minutes.

APPLE BLUEBERRY CRUMBLE

INGREDIENTS

- 5 mL vanilla extract
- 235 mL frozen blueberries
- 5 mL cinnamon
- 1–30 mL brown sugar
- 15 mL lemon juice
- 3 large apples
- 30 mL flour

DIRECTIONS

It's time to turn on the oven and get it to a temperature (of 400F/204C).

Mix the fruit with all of the other ingredients.

Put the topping ingredients in a separate bowl and stir them together.

Put the fruit mixture into a baking dish 8 inches by 8 inches. Spread the topping mixture over the top evenly.

To get a golden brown color, bake for 30 to 45 minutes.

COUNTRYSIDE PASTA TOSS

INGREDIENTS

- 235 mL uncooked rotini pasta (3 ounces)
- 60 mL snap pea pods
- 15 mL chopped fresh parsley
- 225 mL new potatoes, cut into 1/2-inch wedges
- 30 mL butter or margarine
- 80 mL baby-cut carrots
- 1 mL dried dill weed
- 80 mL broccoli florets
- 1 mL salt
- 30 mL fully cooked ham, cut into thin strips

DIRECTIONS

Follow the package instructions for cooking and draining the pasta.

In the meantime, prepare a steaming basket with half an inch of water in a three-quart pot (water should not touch the bottom of the basket). Pack the basket with vegetables like potatoes, broccoli, and carrots. Bring to a boil under a tight cover, then boil the heat to a simmer in the microwave for 5 minutes. Throw in a few pea pods. Stay covered and steam for 2 minutes or until potatoes are fork-tender.

Toss veggies with butter, parsley, dill weed, and salt in a medium bowl until well-covered. The spaghetti and ham should be tossed together after being stirred in.

SPICED ORANGE OLIVE OIL CAKE

INGREDIENTS

- 4 eggs
- 30 mL fresh orange zest
- 350 mL all-purpose flour
- 15 mL baking powder
- 5 mL Chinese five-spice powder
- 177 mL white sugar
- 156 mL extra-virgin olive oil
- 1 pinch salt

DIRECTIONS

Set oven temperature to 350 degrees F. (175 degrees C) to bake. Prepare a loaf pan with some oil and flour.

In a bowl, whisk eggs until they become paler in color. Mix in sugar, olive oil, orange zest, and five-spice powder. Add flour, baking powder, and salt into the egg mixture until combined. Put the batter in the prepared loaf pan.

After 45 minutes in a preheated oven, the cake is made when a toothpick inserted in the middle comes out clean. Allow it cool for 10 minutes in the pan. Take the cake out of the pan and cool it on a rack.

NO-BAKE ENERGY BITES

INGREDIENTS

- 235 mL rolled oats
- 80 mL crunchy peanut butter
- 80 mL honey
- 80 mL miniature semisweet chocolate chips
- 80 mL ground flax seed
- 5 mL vanilla extract

DIRECTIONS

Combine oats, chocolate chips, flax seeds, peanut butter, honey, and vanilla extract in one bowl.

Use your hands to roll out 24 balls of dough. Arrange balls on a baking sheet and freeze until set, about 1 hour.

CHOCOLATE-BANANA TOFU PUDDING

INGREDIENTS

- 75 mL unsweetened cocoa powder
- 355 mL package of soft silken tofu
- 45 mL soy milk
- 1 banana, broken into chunks
- 60 mL confectioners' sugar
- 1 pinch of ground cinnamon

DIRECTIONS

Throw in Cinnamon, sugar, chocolate powder, soy milk, and tofu. Put the lid on it and blend it until it's smooth.

Place in the fridge for at least an hour before serving, then divide into individual serving dishes.

Measurement Conversions

Volume Equivalents (Dry)

US STANDARD	METRIC (APPROXIMATE)
⅛ teaspoon	0.5 mL
¼ teaspoon	1 mL
½ teaspoon	2 mL
¾ teaspoon	4 mL
1 teaspoon	5 mL
1 tablespoon	15 mL
¼ cup	59 mL
⅓ cup	79 mL
½ cup	118 mL
⅔ cup	156 mL
¾ cup	177 mL
1 cup	235 mL
2 cups or 1 pint	475 mL
3 cups	700 mL
4 cups or 1 quart	1 L
½ gallon	2 L
1 gallon	4 L

Volume Equivalents (Liquid)

US STANDARD	US STANDARD (OUNCES)	METRIC (APPROXIMATE)
2 tablespoons	1 fl. oz.	30 mL
¼ cup	2 fl. oz.	60 mL
½ cup	4 fl. oz.	120 mL
1 cup	8 fl. oz.	240 mL
1½ cups	12 fl. oz.	355 mL
2 cups or 1 pint	16 fl. oz.	475 mL
4 cups or 1 quart	32 fl. oz.	1 L
1 gallon	128 fl. oz.	4 L

Oven Temperatures

FAHRENHEIT (F)	CELSIUS (C) (APPROXIMATE)
250°F	120°C
300°F	150°C
325°F	165°C
350°F	180°C
375°F	190°C
400°F	200°C
425°F	220°C
450°F	230°C

Printed in Great Britain
by Amazon

26938420R00051